INFLUENCE OF TECHNOLOGY

- Technology is always evolving and this has an impact on a business's production proces...
- Technology can speed up production an... ...ity.
- Technology can be expensive to incorpo...

Automation	A lot of tasks in factories are now complete... human intervention - less employees...
Computers	Product designs can be produced on a compu... effective and reduces waste but will requir...
Robotics	Robots now complete much of the work on a pr... ...Robo... can work 24/7 and don't need breaks, unlike emplo...

QUALITY

- Quality refers to the standard of a product; ... care and attention put into a product's production...
- Products of higher quality often cost a business more to produce but can command higher selling prices.
- Producing quality products is important to a business as poor quality can lead to...

A Bad Reputation
The business could become known for its low quality products.

Fewer Customers / Sales
Difficult to encourage repeat custom or attract new customers.

Product Returns
Increased numbers of customers returning purchases costs money.

...yees. ...s

ACHIEVING QUALITY

Businesses can achieve quality in two ways:

Quality Assurance

Quality assurance refers to anything a business does before a product is produced to ensure quality. This starts with designing and testing products to ensure that they are fit for purpose and sourcing good quality raw materials, as the final product is likely to reflect the quality of the resources used.

Quality Control

Quality control occurs after a product has been produced. Businesses will take random samples of finished products to check their standard. Batches of finished products might be rejected if quality is poor. Quality control also includes improving processes if quality is regularly less than expected to reduce defective products in future production runs.

SALES

Businesses can sell their products in one of three

E-Commerce	When a business sells its products online. This is becoming increasingly popular with the rise of internet shopping. 
Face to Face	This is when a business's employees make sales to customers in person. 
Telesales	This is when sales are made over the phone, either by appointment or using sales teams to phone selected households. 

E-COMMERCE

- E-commerce is when businesses sell their products online; businesses are now finding they have to adapt to offer some or all of their services online or risk losing out to their competitors.
- E-commerce has these advantages and disadvantages:

✓ Sales can be made 24/7.
✓ Sales can be made worldwide (to new markets).
✓ Less requirement for expensive shop locations and décor.

✗ Cost of website.
✗ Lack of 'impulse buys'.
✗ Greater competition (globally!).
✗ Delivery processes need to be in place / costs involved.

CUSTOMER SERVICE

- Customer service relates to how customers are treated by a business and its employees.
- Good customer service can help a business retain existing customers and attract new customers.
- Businesses can provide customer service through:

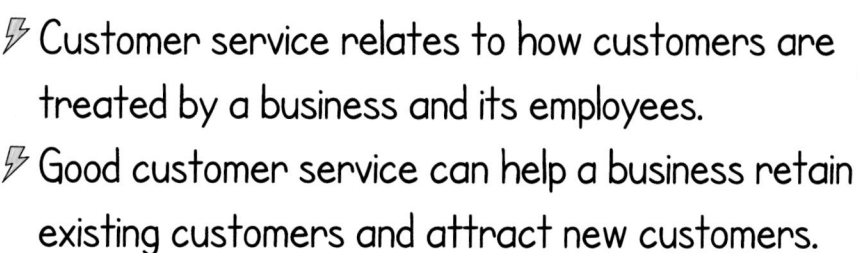

Product Knowledge
Ensuring employees can confidently answer customers' questions about products.

Customer Engagement
Ensuring well presented employees interact politely with customers.

After Sales Service
Offering additional services, such as repairs, after a sale has been secured.

CONSUMER LAW

- Consumers are a business's customers.
- There are laws in place to ensure businesses sell products that are fit for purpose and to ensure customers are protected when making a purchase.
- If businesses do not follow these laws, they risk fines and, for severe law breaches, prison sentences.
- A business that does not comply with consumer laws can also gain poor reviews from customers, leading to a poor reputation and difficultly attracting new customers.

CONSUMER LAWS

Two of the main consumer laws in the UK are:

Consumer Rights Act

Remember this law using its name; it gives consumers rights. This law states that anything a business sells must be as described and fit for purpose (satisfactory quality); so it has to do what the business says it will do! If goods are not, customers have the right to their money back within 30 days of purchase or a repair if it's after 30 days.

Consumer Protection Act

Remember this law using its name; it protects **consumers.** This law states that manufacturers are responsible for any harm caused by their products due to poor quality or poor manufacture. Consumers (or their families) have the right to compensation if a product they have purchased causes damage, personal injury or death.

LOCATION

Businesses have a lot to consider when choosing a place to locate. For some businesses, like those that just operate online, there is less reliance on "passing trade".

Cost
A business will consider monthly rent or the cost to buy premises. Choosing premises in a town or city often costs more.

Proximity to Market
This means how close customers are or how accessible the location is (transport links).

Close to labour
Some businesses rely heavily on skilled employees - they will need to locate near to these employees.

Close to Materials
Businesses that use a lot of raw materials may locate in places with easy access to these materials.

PROCUREMENT

- Procurement involves sourcing goods and services for the business (buying!). This could be raw materials or services, such as maintenance and cleaning.

- Procurement roles involve:

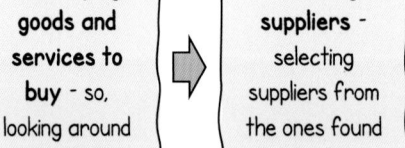

Identifying goods and services to buy - so, looking around and finding suppliers.

→ **Choosing suppliers** - selecting suppliers from the ones found (best price/ quality).

→ **Ordering** - procurement staff are responsible for making orders of goods and services.

→ **Receiving deliveries** - staff will manage where and when deliveries are required.

SUPPLY DECISIONS

- Businesses have to make a lot of decisions to ensure they get supplies to where they need to be and to ensure these arrive on time (this is called **logistics**).
- If they do not make these decisions carefully, a whole production line could be held up, costing them money.
- Poor quality supplies will likely lead to poor quality final products, which could lead to a poor reputation for a business and also product returns, which will cost them money.

SUPPLY DECISIONS

Time

Does the business want to hold a lot of supplies (stock) with the expense of storing it or risk delivery methods like **Just in Time** (JIT), where products are delivered when they are required?

Supply Chain

This is the number of businesses raw materials pass through to reach their final destination. A longer supply chain involves more businesses and more risk of something going wrong.

Reliability

Businesses need to be sure they choose reliable suppliers. If they are not reliable in terms of time and quality, then the business's whole production process may need to pause or quality could be compromised.

Costs

Businesses need to choose suppliers carefully. They may not necessarily go for the cheapest supplier, but need to find the balance of cost compared to the quality of supplies they are provided with.

THE FINANCE FUNCTION

- The finance functional area (department) deals with the business's money. It manages cash flow (money coming in and out) and produces financial reports.
- The finance function also make important business decisions based on money; e.g. what supplies the business can afford.
- All other functional areas (departments) will be set a budget by the finance function, this is to help stop the business from over-spending.

FINANCE

- Finance refers to money.
- Businesses need money (finance) for:

Setting up their business initially.	Funding expansion and new product development.	Running the business on a daily basis.	Recruitment (adverts etc.).	Marketing, in order to increase sales.

- Where money comes from is called a source of finance:

Loan	For large purchases. Money from banks. Interest is charged.
Overdraft	Arranging to go below £0 with the bank. For short-term finance.

OTHER SOURCES OF FINANCE

Trade Credit	Suppliers deliver goods and request payment at a later date.
Retained Profit	When established businesses keep profit back to use in future.
Sale of Assets	Selling assets, such as machinery and vehicles.
Owners' Capital	When owners, such as sole traders, invest more of their money.
New Partner	When partnerships invite a new partner to join (bringing capital).
Share Issue	When limited companies release more shares for sale.
Crowdfunding	Asking people to donate money online in return for discounts/gifts.

REVENUE

Revenue is the name given to money made from sales.

Selling Price x Number Sold

Silly Sox sell each pair of socks to clothing stores worldwide for £2.50.

To calculate revenue for 5000 pairs of Silly Sox...

£2.50 x 5000 = **£12,500 Revenue**

So that's £2.50 selling price for each pair of socks multiplied by the number sold over a given time (5000).

BUSINESS COSTS

- A cost is something a business must pay in order to operate.
- Costs can be grouped as fixed or variable.

Fixed costs do not change with output. These costs still have to be paid even if the business doesn't make/sell any products.

Total **variable costs** will change depending on how many products a business manufactures. These costs will be £0 if no products are made.

FIXED COSTS

- Fixed costs stay the same no matter how many products a business manufactures.
- The below scenario highlights some fixed costs:

Silly Sox  manufactures socks from cotton for sale to clothing stores around the world.

Silly Sox will have these fixed costs...

Rent; the factory rent stays the same each month.

Insurance; insurance is the same, regardless of output.

Loan repayments; these are fixed monthly payments.

VARIABLE COSTS

- Total variable costs usually increase when a business manufactures / sells more products.
- The below scenario highlights some variable costs:

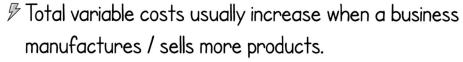

Silly Sox manufactures socks from cotton for sale to clothing stores around the world.

Silly Sox will have these variable costs...

Raw Materials; more socks made = more cotton.

Components; more socks = more elastic etc.

Packaging; more socks made = more labels/packets.

TOTAL COSTS

Total costs are fixed and variable costs added together:

Fixed Costs + Total Variable Costs

Silly Sox has fixed costs of £2,600 and variable costs of £1.20 per pair of socks made.

To calculate total costs for 5000 pairs of Silly Sox...

£2,600 + (£1.20 x 5000) = **£8,600**

So that's £1.20 variable cost per pair multiplied by 5000 pairs, then add the fixed costs of £2,600.

PROFIT OR LOSS?

- Profit is the money left from revenue after costs have been paid (so it's **revenue minus costs**). If costs are higher than revenue, the business will be making a **loss**.
- Businesses need to monitor their profit in order to help inform decision making.
- A business making a large profit might want to invest in new product development or expansion, unlike a business making a small profit. A business making a loss may need to take action to avoid going bankrupt.

PROFIT

- There are two types of profit.
- **Gross profit** is calculated using this formula:

In this formula, **cost of sales** are the costs directly involved in making the product. So, if the product were a cake, the ingredients.

Revenue - Cost of Sales

- **Net profit** is calculated using this formula:

In this formula, **expenses** are the additional costs the business incurred such as rent, electricity, gas etc.

Gross Profit - Expenses

PROFIT EXAMPLES

Gross Profit

- Silly Sox sold 5000 pairs of socks. These were sold for £2.50 each generating **revenue of £12,500** (5000 x £2.50).
- Each pair directly cost £1.20 to make (raw materials, components and packaging), totalling £6,000.
- Silly Sox have a **Gross Profit of £6,500** (£12,500 revenue - £6,000 cost of sales).

Net Profit

- Silly Sox had expenses of £2,600 including their rent, insurance and loan repayment.
- Silly Sox have a **Net Profit of £3,900** (£6,500 gross profit - £2,600 expenses).

PROFITABILITY RATIOS

- A profitability ratio shows how profitable a business is based on the revenue they have made.
- These are used because a business can have a high revenue but make a low profit or even a loss!
- These ratios show, for every £1 a business makes in revenue, how much of that is profit.

Gross Profit Margin

$$\frac{\text{Gross Profit}}{\text{Total Revenue}} \times 100$$

Net Profit Margin

$$\frac{\text{Net Profit}}{\text{Total Revenue}} \times 100$$

PROFITABILITY RATIOS IN ACTION

Gross Profit Margin

$$\frac{\text{Gross Profit}}{\text{Total Revenue}} \times 100 \qquad \frac{6{,}500}{12{,}500} \times 100 = 52\%$$

So, for every £1 of revenue, 52p is gross profit.

Net Profit Margin

$$\frac{\text{Net Profit}}{\text{Total Revenue}} \times 100 \qquad \frac{3{,}900}{12{,}500} \times 100 = 31.2\%$$

And for every £1 of revenue, 31p is net profit.

AVERAGE RATE OF RETURN

- Average rate of return (ARR) shows how much money a business can expect to get back from an investment.
- Businesses use this calculation to determine if an investment is worthwhile - it will compare investments using this formula to help with decision making.
- To calculate Average Rate of Return:

$$\textbf{Average Rate of Return (\%)} = \frac{\text{Average Profit from Investment}}{\text{Cost of Investment}} \times 100$$

AVERAGE RATE OF RETURN

- These calculations need to be completed in order to calculate average rate of return using the formula above!

Total Profit from Investment = Total Income from Investment − Total Cost of Investment

$$\textbf{Average Profit from Investment} = \frac{\text{Total Profit from Investment}}{\text{Number of Years of Investment}} \times 100$$

BREAK-EVEN

- Break-even is the point at which a business has covered its costs but is not yet making a profit.

- So, at this point, revenue is equal to total costs.
- Break-even is given as a number of products/sales.
- Break-even can be calculated with this formula:

$$\frac{\text{Fixed Costs}}{\text{Selling Price - Variable Cost per Unit}}$$

Do this part of the calculation first! → (Selling Price - Variable Cost per Unit)

BREAK-EVEN

- Break-even is useful for a business so they know how many product sales to aim for to start making a profit.
- Break-even is given as a number of products.
- Break-even has its limits; it is based on one single selling price and it doesn't factor in temporary price changes.

To calculate Silly Soxs' break-even point:

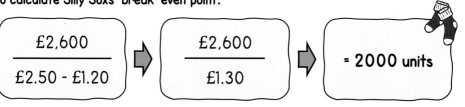

$$\frac{£2,600}{£2.50 - £1.20} \rightarrow \frac{£2,600}{£1.30} \rightarrow = \textbf{2000 units}$$

CASH

- Cash is vital to a business's operations. A business may have made a large number of sales but could still become 'insolvent' if it does not have cash to pay its short-term debts and expenses.
- Cash is different to profit; profit is the money left over when costs have been paid.
- Cash flow refers to money coming into and out of a business. If more goes out than is coming in, a business could be in trouble - especially if this is for a long period.

CASH FLOW FORECASTS

A cash flow forecast is a document used to plan for money coming into and out of a business. These documents help businesses identify periods of cash shortages so they can put plans in place to cover these.

	Aug	Sept	Oct
Opening Balance	1000	1300	2000
Total Inflows	500	800	700
Total Outflows	200	100	500
Closing Balance	1300	2000	2200

Opening Balance = Last month's closing balance.

Opening Balance + inflows - outflows gives closing balance.

Inflows - Outflows = Net Cash flow

ETHICS

- If a business tries to operate ethically, they try to operate fairly and with consideration to people and the environment.
- A business operating ethically aims to treat people right, including these stakeholders...

Workers
Paying employees fair wages and treating them well. This will increase employee retention.

Customers
Not "rip off" customers by charging too much or knowingly selling inadequate products.

Suppliers
Paying fair amounts for products and using supplies such as "Fairtrade".

ETHICS

- Operating ethically can also involve sourcing materials carefully; checking where supplies come from.
- Operating ethically does cost businesses extra resources but operating ethically can improve a business's reputation.
- Businesses that do not operate ethically can get negative attention (media/reviews) and some customers will choose to go to competitors instead (loss of sales/money).

THE ENVIRONMENT

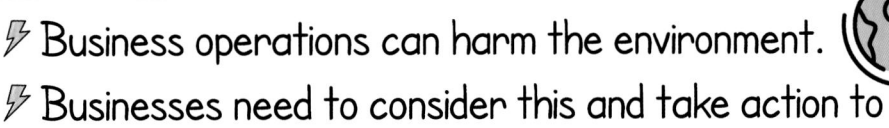

- Business operations can harm the environment.
- Businesses need to consider this and take action to reduce their impact on the environment.
- Businesses must consider...

All these can improve brand image!

Sustainability
Can the resources they use be replaced? Use less fossil fuels and replenish natural resources (trees).

Waste Disposal
Businesses should aim to reduce waste and recycle any waste they do generate.

Pollution
Businesses should aim to reduce the pollution (air/water/noise) that they generate.

Climate Change
Businesses may aim to reduce their carbon footprint and reduce their emissions (less transport etc.).

ECONOMIC CLIMATE

Economic climate refers to how stable an economy is; so, how many people are in work, how readily are people spending and how confident are businesses in developing new product ideas?

Levels of Consumer Income

Lower levels of consumer income means people generally have less to spend and may avoid purchases of non-essential or branded items. This will have an impact on a business's sales, particularly those selling "luxury" items.

Unemployment

High unemployment again means that people will have less to spend in general. This can impact on sales and profits. There will, however, be more people available if the business needs to recruit new employees; so, more choice.

GLOBALISATION

- Increasingly, businesses are operating globally and there are now a large number of brands that are recognised around the world. This is called Globalisation - we have less "local" businesses and life is becoming increasingly "standard", regardless of where we live.
- Globalisation is due to:

Improvements in communication (internet).	Cheaper and more frequent worldwide travel.	The growth of multinational companies.	Greater trade deals between countries.

IMPACT OF GLOBALISTION

- Globalisation means that small businesses can struggle as they face competition from multinational companies.
- Businesses may also struggle because customers can purchase products from anywhere in the world.
- Businesses can, however, choose where they want to locate, especially if they operate fully online. This can reduce their costs if locating in cheaper countries.
- Globalisation is contributing to individual countries and cultures losing some of their identity.

INTERDEPENDENCE

Departments within a business are interdependent; they depend on one another.

Finance link with...

All departments - to set budgets.
All departments - avoiding overspending.
All departments - what can be afforded?

Operations link with...

Finance - what do supplies cost?
Marketing - what does research say?
Human Resources - employee training.

Marketing link with...

Finance - what marketing can we afford?
Human Resources - we need employees!
Operations - what products do we promote?

Human Resources link with...

Finance - what staff can we afford?
Marketing - what staff do you need?
Operations - health and safety compliance.

BUSINESS DECISIONS

- A business's functional areas depend on one another and they are constantly communicating between one another as part of a business's daily operations.
- Big decisions, however, will require all functional areas to work together and have an input.

Decision: Planning a Takeover

Finance - can we afford it? Will it work?
Human Resources - extra staff needed?
Marketing - does research support this?
Operations - sharing resources/supplies.

Decision: Launching a New Product

Finance - what will the costs be?
Human Resources - staff training?
Marketing - how can we promote it?
Operations - planning the new product.

RISK AND REWARD

- Businesses need to ensure they make wise decisions; risks need to be considered before decisions are made.
- Shareholders of a company vote on a big decisions; they need to be convinced the reward outweighs the potential risks involved if they are to agree!
- Not taking risks can be a risk in itself though! For example, Blockbuster™ famously turned down an offer to buy Netflix™ for $50 million. Blockbuster™ now no longer trades and Netflix™ is worth billions.